NETTE HILTON is an established author of children's literature and has won several awards for her books, which range from early childhood stories to novels for older readers. Her work includes the forever popular *Proper Little Lady* and *The Web*, both of which have won awards and have been translated into many languages.

Nette's work, although predominantly for children of all ages, includes three adult thrillers. She writes from the NSW north coast where she shares her life with dogs, an ageing cat and other feathered beasts. She continues to fuel her imagination by working part-time at a primary school. This career, which has spanned 34 years, places her at the coalface of changing ideas and understandings of what it is to be a child in the new millennium. She doesn't confess to being a guru on child development but it certainly helps in putting together a very readable and fun book.

Her work beyond teaching and writing includes regular workshops and author talks at many writing venues, including literature festivals that occur around the country.

Other books by Nette Hilton

Woolly Jumpers
Grave Catastrophe
The Smallest Bilby and The Midnight Star
The Web
Little Platypus

NETTE HILTON

Star of the Show

ILLUSTRATED BY
CHANTAL STEWART

First published 2006 by University of Queensland Press
PO Box 6042, St Lucia, Queensland 4067 Australia

www.uqp.uq.edu.au

Typeset by Peripheral Vision
Set in 11/16pt Stempel Garamond
Printed in Australia by McPherson's Printing Group

Cataloguing-in-Publication Data
National Library of Australia
Hilton, Nette, 1946-.
 Star of the show.

 For lower to middle primary school children.

 I. Christmas plays - Juvenile fiction. I. Title.
 I. Stewart, Chantal. II. Title.

A823.3

ISBN 0 7022 3579 2.

Chapter One

It's not fair.

I've put up with Serena Sweetmay all my life. I've put up with her in preschool when everyone used to say how lovely she was. And how polite.

I've put up with her in Year 1 when she got picked to present the flowers to the lady who came from the Council. Serena got to hand them over in front of the whole town and everyone clapped and cheered and said how lovely she looked in her little blue dress.

It was enough to make you sick.

I've put up with her in Year 2 when she was chosen to dance in the front line of the concert in a lollipop dress with big bobbly buttons on the front.

Everyone clapped and cheered and the rest of us in our brown chocolate lolly wrappers didn't even get noticed. We were supposed to be the funny ones.

I've put up with her in Year 3 when she wore her golden curls tugged up in a ponytail that tumbled down her back and showed off the dimples in her soft, pink cheeks. She smiled a lot in Year 3 because Mr Phillips told her she was the only girl he'd ever taught with dimples in her cheeks. I reckoned he should have filled them with blu-tak. She never smiled at us unless she wanted something, like a visit to our granny's if our granny lived in a good place with a swimming pool or something.

And now, I have to put up with her coming to my place on Saturday afternoon.

'How come?'

'Don't be like that, Aimee,' Mum said while she zipped around trying to get our lunches into their lunchboxes and shoes on Roly's feet at the same time. Roly's only two and goes to daycare while Mum's at work. I don't think it's very hygienic pushing sandwiches with one hand and Roly's foot with the other. 'Here, finish doing your lunches while I fix Roly.'

I packed the boxes and put a couple of extra roll-ups in mine for recess. 'One of those will be quite enough, Aimee.'

Chapter One

I reckon my mum's got eyes in the back of her head.

I took one out. 'How come Serena's coming on Saturday?'

'Because she is.' She said. 'I know she can be a bit tricky but it's not for long. Heavens, you've been in the same classes forever. Surely one more afternoon isn't going to make too much difference.'

I wished I could send her somewhere else.

For most of the year in Year Four Serena has been sent off to deliver messages or take visitors to the office. Sometimes I think Miss Everest is glad to get rid of her—she sends her on so many errands.

Serena doesn't think so. 'She'll always choose me,' she said when Javin reckoned it was time for him to have a turn. He never gets chosen because he never comes back. 'I always remember to knock and say "excuse me" and smile, and I always get the message right. It makes Miss Everest look good.'

I thought Miss Everest looked good anyway, except for the days when she's bawling out Javin, but she doesn't do it for very long. And her cheeks look nice when they're all red.

'My mother's a teacher,' Serena said when I told her Miss Everest was all right. 'And so I know the way teachers think.'

'She drives me nuts,' I told Mum, who'd dumped

Roly on the floor and was tearing around trying to find her keys. 'N.U.T.S.'

I made a couple of loopy circles around my ears and lolled my tongue out one side of my mouth.

Roly shrieked. I crossed my eyes and made drooling noises.

Roly shrieked a little louder.

Chapter One

'Come on, you two,' Mum said, skidding us out the door and into the car. Dad walked around the side of the house to help her bundle us in. He left the car that he was getting ready to sell standing with its bonnet open like a patient waiting for the dentist to start drilling.

'Have a good day, you lot.' He grinned when I

told him about the car being in a dentist's chair. 'That car will have its teeth fixed in time for Christmas,' he said. 'And then we'll have enough money for something super special!'

'I'll believe it when I see it,' Mum said, but she was laughing. She checked her hair in the rear-vision mirror and then checked that her lipstick was okay. She blew Dad a kiss and smoothed her supermarket uniform over the seat away from Roly's feet. 'Thank goodness it's Friday.' She sighed as we bumped out of our driveway and onto the road. 'Just one more day and we're home for the whole weekend.'

It definitely wasn't fair.

Mum works most weekends and this one, when she was going to be home for the two whole days, I was going to have to share part of it with Serena stupid Sweetmay.

'I don't want her to come over,' I said before I could stop myself.

Mum glanced at me in the rear-vision mirror. 'Don't start again, Aimee. Surely you can get along for one afternoon. Her mother asked me specially.'

'Why can't she go to Angela or Katie's house?' I grumbled. 'She's always with them at school.'

'Because her dad's calling in with some work for Dad and her mum has to go up to Brisbane. It was easier for Serena to come with him to our house.

Chapter One

Now, give it a rest.'

I didn't want to give it a rest. I wanted to howl and complain all the way to town. Mum checked me in the rear-vision again and I could see it would be best if I didn't. Her eyes are green but they're especially green and witchy when she's starting to get fed up.

I clamped my arms across my chest and scowled out at the world instead.

Serena Sweetmay is a pain.

P.A.I.N.

'Oh, come on,' Mum said, as she tipped me out of the car at the school gate. 'It's just one teensy-tiny afternoon … and we'll all go and get a hamburger for dinner to help you get over it.'

We hardly ever have hamburgers. Ever.

The pain eased enough for me to tickle Roly goodbye and blow Mum a kiss. It was only for a couple of hours, after all.

Surely I could handle that.

Chapter Two

'Well, now. Let me look at you.' Miss Everest is always really pleased to see us. It's like she hasn't seen us in ever so long and she's really happy we all happened to be here at the same time. 'How's the best singing class in the whole school today?'

A little ripple of excitement drifted right down our line. We grinned at each other.

'Did we get it?'

'Did they choose us?'

'Did they? Did they? Tell us, Miss Everest. Pleeease.'

Miss Everest just grinned back at us.

'Not until you're all sitting neat and quiet on the

Chapter Two

mat inside,' she said.

We all scrambled up the steps and tried to shove our bags into their right places. Most of us tried, anyway. Javin never bothers. He just leaves his where it lands and we all climb over it or across it.

'Pick it up, Javin,' Miss Everest said.

We all waited while Javin acted as if he didn't know how his bag could possibly be in the middle of the floor all squashed, before he decided to collect it. He complained for a while about having nowhere to put it, but Miss Everest is good at ignoring him, sometimes, and had already started to tell us the exciting news.

'We won,' she said. 'We're the class that's going to do the school Christmas play this year. We're it!'

We all hooted and howled and Javin did a little hoo-hoo-hoo dance that made him look like he was stirring an enormous pot of heavy stew. George and Edward rolled into a big heap in the middle of the floor and would have kicked their legs in the air except that Miss Everest had already stood up and they could see it wasn't going to be their best idea yet.

'Don't forget to thank Mr Henderson when you see him in the playground. If he hadn't helped us with the songs and all the words we mightn't have been so good.'

I think Miss Everest is keen on Mr Henderson. She's always a bit breathy when she says his name, as if she's suddenly filled up with a giant thrill. She stands close to him as well. And he's always dropping in with his guitar to see how the best class in the school is going.

And then he stands in the corner and talks to the best class's teacher.

'How come his class didn't get it then?' Edward called out. He thinks he's pretty smart.

'Too young,' Miss Everest said. 'It has to be a primary class, not one of the kindy classes.'

'Bit weird him having a kindy class if you ask me,' Edward said. 'Blokes are better with the big kids.'

'*Some* blokes are better with big kids, Edward, and we didn't ask you.'

Miss Everest waited until we had all settled down again. It always takes a while, because Javin likes to sit in about six different places before Miss Everest makes him come and sit by her. By that time Edward and George had moved as well, but we jammed up tight so they couldn't keep moving. We wanted to hear about the Christmas play.

'We're all going to have a part in it. And we're all going to dress up. And we're all going to sing all the songs and ... best of all ...'

We held our breath.

Chapter Two

Miss Everest waited until we were almost exploding from holding our breaths.

'What?' Jasmin cried when she couldn't stand it any longer.

'There's going to be a special visitor in the audience. A friend of Mr Henderson's who makes commercials ...'

'Real commercials?'

'Like on tele?'

'Commercials can be on the radio as well ...'

'And in the paper ...'

Miss Everest held up her hand. 'Television commercials,' she said.

I could imagine it straightaway.

I could imagine me being a television commercial star. I'd be just like Susie Donovan from the Pixels, who wears lovely swirling giant skirts and true high heels and lipstick and her hair is so curled it bounces like golden springs all around her shoulders. She's a pop star now and often has her photo in Girlfriend. I saw a film about her making her newest singing video and she was dancing with a boy who was tall and had long, strong arms and spun her around close to him and then whooshed his arms around her middle.

My hair is straight and gets a bit straggly when it grows longer than my shoulders. Mum says it would look better if we got it trimmed, but I'm growing it really, really long and there's no way we're cutting any of it off until it reaches down to the middle of my back.

My legs are a bit skinny too. Skinnier that Susie Dovovan's anyway, but I could always wear long floaty dresses that covered them so it'd be fine. Swirling giant skirts would be okay as well, as long as they came down past my knees. High heels were going to help no end.

I dressed myself in my dreams and danced my way across the stage with the cameras rolling to the tall boy with spiky blonde hair who was waiting for me.

'Aimee?'

I heard a few sniggers around me. Jasmin gave me poke with her elbow. Javin pinged a bit of paper at me. I hoped he hadn't spat on it to make it go further.

'Wake up.' Miss Everest was handing me my maths sheets. 'Time for our tables test.'

I dreamed back to my seat. All around me I could hear kids whispering about our Christmas play and the special visitor and how they'd be able to pick him out.

'Bet he'll wear dark glasses,' I heard George say to Jimmy.

Jimmy looked a bit worried. He's not too sure about things the first time he hears them.

'It's at night time,' Jimmy said. 'He won't be able to see.'

George buried his head in his maths test so he wouldn't have to get into explaining it all to Jimmy.

I leaned over to turn his page to the one we had to do. Jimmy always starts in the wrong place.

I could hear Serena whispering. She leaned closer to Angela and Katie but her voice was loud enough to be sure our table could hear too.

'It's just the way teachers talk,' she was saying.

'They think it'll make us perform better if they tell us there'll be someone special watching us. I know,' she added when she was sure we were all listening in, 'because my mother's a teacher.'

She might have been right. I didn't know.

What I did know was that I wanted to be the star of the show. Just once I wanted to be the one that everyone noticed.

And clapped. And cheered.

But what chance would I have?

Who was ever, ever going to do that while Serena Sweetmay was on the same stage?

Chapter Three

I put on my long aqua velvet skirt and my puffy-sleeved white blouse and sat on the verandah in the sun. I put on my white summer sandals because they were the only shoes that I had with a little bit of a heel. My feet had grown since last summer but not too much. My toes only poked over the end a bit, but the straps were tight and my littlest toe kept popping itself free like a jack-in-the-box who'd been boxed for too long.

'You'll trip over in those shoes,' Mum said, while she bundled Roly into his car seat to take him to do the grocery shopping. I wasn't sorry I wasn't heading off with her. Doing anything in a shopping centre with Roly was a bit dodgy, especially if it involved food.

'No, I won't,' I said.

Dad hurried along the verandah behind me. He's got a little office at the end that he built for himself. He keeps his art work in there and all his designs for his surfboards. He's a great artist, but it doesn't make a lot of money so he has to keep fixing up cars until he's more famous.

'I'll get the stroller,' he called out.

The floorboards dipped and swayed with each footstep and I felt like I was floating. I wished he'd keep walking up and down forever.

I leaned back and watched the shine of the sun on the deep plush of my old velvet skirt. Bits of velvet have worn off in some places, but down the legs it almost shimmered in the light. I lifted my feet in their white sandals and pointed my toes.

I let my head arch back like they do in the commercials on tele when they're trying to sell chocolates. I imagined my hair drifting down onto the floorboards and fanning out in a shell shape under my shoulders.

'You'll get a cramp,' Dad said as he thumped by again.

The floorboards rocked me and I leaned further back and draped my arm above my shell-shaped hair.

Chapter Three

I heard Mum's car leave and the rustle of Dad's surf designs as he set them up on the easels ready for Serena's dad.

I dreamed of the boy with spiky hair who was going to catch me as I soared through the air and into his arms. I thought it might look better if I was skating, so I rebuilt the dream and this time I had on long white skating boots and I was drifting across the ice.

I raised my arms and gave myself a little push so I was sitting up, leaning out with my arms forming a circle in front of me. I gazed down into it as if it were filled with downy, yellow chicks all cheeping and looking back up at me.

I twirled one small step with them out onto the grass. Not one chick fell, but they looked a bit surprised to be twirling around on ice and their heads all looped a bit to one side and they began to climb on top of each other before I could stop them, so I had to pause for a moment and change the chicks into a soft spaniel puppy.

I rocked it back and forth.

I pointed my toes when I rocked.

'What are you doing?'

The puppy landed with a splat on the ice and I almost bent over to right it, but I stopped myself and pretended to be brushing away some creases that had formed in my blouse.

'Hi, Serena,' I said.

'Hello, Serena.' Dad stepped off the verandah and onto the lawn beside me. 'You're looking pretty grown-up.'

She was.

She had on a pair of tight jeans that sat down low on her hips and had a checked cuff that snugged around her calves. She must have more hip than me, because my jeans still fall down if I don't have them higher up with some elastic in the back. Her shoes were proper leather clogs with a thick sole that made her look really tall. And her hair was tied in a ponytail that sat on the back of her neck and hung, long and golden and curly, right down to the middle of her back.

'Hello, Aimee. That's a super skirt you're wearing,' Serena's dad said. 'Did your mum make it for you?'

I just looked at it and smiled.

Dad was shaking hands with Dave, Serena's dad. 'She sure did,' he said and grinned at me. 'She made some muesli crunch and left it in the kitchen for you and Serena as well.'

'Muesli crunch?' said Serena. 'Ew. What's that?'

'It's delicious,' said Dad as he steered Dave up onto the verandah and down towards his little office. I was pretty sure Dave would have had a proper door on his office and wished that Dad's door wasn't just an old door that he'd found up the coast and cut in half so he could have the top open and the bottom shut to keep Roly out. 'Don't eat too much though. We don't want you popping out of your jeans before you get home.'

Dave laughed.

Serena didn't. She waved her hand above the verandah floor to frighten away any dust and then sat on the very, very edge.

'Let's go sit inside so we don't get dirty,' she said.

I took Serena inside. She wandered through our lounge room looking at the walls and the pictures and the desk and the lounge and the cushions that Mum had made.

'How come you've got a desk in the lounge room,' she said. She ambled closer and picked up a little cannon that Dad had found. She turned it over and put it back down while I was still trying to think of a reason why we had a desk in the lounge room.

'Where's your room?'

I'd tidied my room specially and Mum had put my Barbie bedspread on the bed. It has a matching pillowslip and a pink frill that sits under the mattress so you can't see the junk under the bed.

'Do you still play with Barbie?' Serena said. She

20

smoothed a spot and then sat down. 'I haven't played with Barbie for years.'

My Barbie dolls were sitting on the shelf that Dad had put up for them last year. I still love my Flying Barbie even though I haven't given her a good fly for a long time. She has the loveliest wings that shine like oil when you spill it across water.

'My gran sends them to me,' I lied.

Serena had opened my cupboard doors. She was looking at the clothes hanging in the wardrobe. 'What's that?' she said.

I peered in behind her. It was an old sari that my mum had bought when she visited India before I was born. Before she even met Dad. It's a beautiful pale blue with soft silver threads all around the bottom and twisted petals and flowers twining themselves in and out around the edges.

I told Serena about it and we pulled it out. She wrapped it around herself and trailed it behind her over to the mirror.

'It smells a bit, doesn't it?' she said.

'It's dust. And incense that Mum used to burn whenever she wore it.'

Serena let the sari fall. She stepped over it and wandered back out to the lounge room.

'Look at that,' she said and pointed to the crack in the wall where the chimney doesn't quite meet.

'Why's that like that?'

'The timber's shrunk,' I said. 'It's okay, though. Nothing will happen.'

'Things could crawl through that,' Serena said.

I was going to tell her that only very skinny things would crawl through there and what would it matter anyway? Whatever wanted to come in would come in through the doors or the windows or down the chimney with Santa if necessary. But I didn't bother. Dad reckons it's a special celebration marker, because the sun shines through there only at a particular time of the year and that's when we have to run around the yard chanting made-up songs and make wishes. We write our wishes with white pens on silver paper and burn them in a little brass bowl.

Serena was touching things and lifting bits and pieces on the desk, like she was in the bargain centre of the Dollar Shop.

She opened the lid of a box that held my dad's drawing pastels. She chose one and scribbled a little line on a piece of scrap paper. 'I suppose we could do some drawing. Have you got any paper?'

I was glad she'd finally found something that we could do together.

'I have to ask Dad if we can use his pastels.'

We went up the verandah to the office. Serena stepped carefully as if she was scared she might disappear through the bendy verandah boards at any second.

'Excuse me,' she said in a soft, lispy voice. 'Could we please use your drawing pastels, Mr Appleshore. We'd be really, really careful.'

Serena batted her eyelashes at Dad and folded her hands into a little boat in front of her.

'Sorry, Serena,' Dad said. 'They're strictly for my use only, but ...' He leaned over his desk and lifted out a shoebox. 'There's a whole lot of stumps and bits and pieces of colour in here, and Aimee has some nice pencil sets in her room. Why not use them?'

I raced back along the verandah and get the set of 500 colours that Mum had bought for me from the Dollar Shop. They cost more than a dollar but they were excellent value, Mum said, at five dollars. I got my crayons as well. And some glitter sticks and my glue and glitter stars.

'We can draw our costumes for the Christmas play,' I said. 'I'm going to be an angel.'

Serena looked at me as if I was nuts.

'That's nice. I think I'm going to be an angel as well.' She smiled. 'So are Angela and Katie.'

I'd have a chance if it were only Angela and Katie.

I smiled back and bent closer to my paper and drew a border around the edge with stars and halos and little clouds in it. I wasn't smiling inside and I think my halos were a little bit yellower than halos should be. And they dug into the page a bit as well, but my fingers were hanging on so tight to the pencil I couldn't seem to help it.

Serena Sweetmay got chosen for everything.

I glanced up at her. Her face was soft and round and pink-cheeked. Her eyelashes curved onto the face in a long, luscious wave. Her hair let little drifty bits go so they curled onto her forehead and in little wisps down in front of her ears.

Her lips were rosebudded and shiny, although I think she'd been using some lip gloss to make them as shiny as that.

Everyone, everyone, everyone beamed on Serena Sweetmay.

Even people who didn't know her chose her to do things. The bloke who turned up with the puppet show and a set of big drums didn't know her. He'd never seen her and he chose her out of about five hundred kids. He chose Javin too, but that was because Miss Everest had already moved Javin to the front and the bloke had tripped over him trying to get to Serena.

It wouldn't have mattered so much if she'd messed up. It would have been great if she'd blooped on the tuba and fallen over the drum kit or slapped when she should have slammed, but she didn't. She never, ever does.

Even when the tuba made a noise like a constipated elephant she managed to smile sweetly and all the adults for miles around thought how lovely she was.

Yuk!

I started drawing my angel. I gave her dark hair like mine and long skinny legs. And enormous wings made out of lots of little thin lines so they looked like feathers.

I dreamed my angel as I drew.

I dreamed me being my angel as I drew.

As I drew a white fluffy cloud for my angel to stand on, I glanced over at Serena's sheet.

Her angel wasn't anywhere near as good as mine. She's not an artist and her faces and bodies are always wrong.

I didn't kid myself that it would make a scrap of difference.

Whether Serena could draw an angel or not wasn't going to make a scrap of difference. If Serena decided she wanted to be one, we could all be sure she was going to get chosen.

It mightn't make her the star of the show though.

I drew a big star on top of my angel. I rubbed it for luck, but it didn't make me feel a whole lot better.

Being a star on the same stage as Serena Sweetmay was going to take a bit more than luck.

Chapter Four

I told Mum all about the Christmas play when we were putting the groceries away. Roly had curled up on the couch and gone to sleep. Mum said he wore himself out trying to get out of his stroller. She looked pretty worn out as well.

She leaned on the bench and had a break while I told her all about it.

'I loved being in plays when I was little,' she said. 'I was a blind man once.'

I wasn't sure how excited I'd be if my role was a blind man.

'I can't wait,' she said. 'What do you want to be?'

'An angel.'

She went back to stacking tins into the cupboard, but I could tell she was thinking about it. The tins looked like skittles by the time she'd finished. They usually just land where she's shoved them.

'Doesn't everyone always want to be the angel?' she said. 'There's always heaps of them. Don't you want to be something different?'

Chapter Four

I didn't want to be different. I wanted to be the angel.

I picked up the bag of carrots and started packing them into the fridge tray. I packed them carefully so they'd fit without jamming against the shelf, but I only saw the angel that was going to be me in the play.

I was going to be in the middle of the bench at the back and I was going to have a halo that was gold and

sparkling, and my wings were going to be the sort that had real feathers glued onto each other so they fanned out like an eagle's wings. Only they'd be white with gold trims and not brown and grey like an eagle.

'Where do you buy angels' wings?' I said. 'The ones with feathers on them.'

'New or used?' Dad joked from the doorway.

I ignored him.

'I guess it would depend if you've got any Fly-Buys?' He chortled to himself. My dad thinks he's really funny when he gets going.

'And I guess you'd have to get permission from the Wing Commander,' he went on. 'Or the Flight Lieutenant.'

Mum shushed him. She was trying not to laugh though.

'I'm not sure,' she said, as she rolled potatoes into the dish in the cupboard. 'We could make them, I guess.'

I didn't want ones made at home. Serena wouldn't have made ones. Or Angela or Katie.

'Your dad could make some in no time, couldn't you, Dan?'

'Couldn't I what?' Dad finished putting the shopping bags away and joined in again.

'Make some wings for Aimee's angel outfit?'

Chapter Four

I wanted him to say no. But he was leaning against the fridge and he had his fingers against his mouth like when he's planning a new design.

'What sort of wings? Big, small, wide, narrow? Feathers?'

'The bought kind,' I said. 'With long, long, soft feathers with gold tips on them.'

'No worries,' said Dad.

I was worried though.

'They have to be really long.' I drew big hoop shapes with my hands that reached down to my hips. 'And not too heavy. And with gold tips.'

Roly started to grizzle from the lounge room.

'I know just what you mean.' Dad winked as he wandered out to collect Roly and didn't say another word.

He fetched his drawing book and sat with it and didn't look up at the tele. Not once.

When I peeked over to have a look, I saw angels' wings.

Long and feathery and he'd even twiddled little lines at their edges.

Gold tips.

Chapter Five

Miss Everest had cleared a big space in the middle of our classroom. She'd pushed all the desks into little groups against the walls so we could spread out and start to get ready for our play.

'Now,' she said as she curled her feet up under her. Serena said it sets a bad example, but Miss Everest always kicks her shoes off before she puts them on the chair. 'Let's get organised. I want angels in one group, shepherds in another, wise men over there, an innkeeper, a Joseph and a Mary, and the manger cow and a sheep group.'

There were a lot of angels and wise men, a couple of shepherds, five innkeepers, seven Josephs, five Marys, and nobody in the manger cow and sheep group.

'Oh dear.' Miss Everest held up the two ends of the manger cow outfit. 'We really have to use this. Poor Mr Dean will be so upset if we don't.'

Mr Dean is the old codger who comes in to help Jimmy with his reading. I don't know where Miss Everest found him, but Javin reckons it was probably out at the cemetery.

'Hanging around waiting to get in, most likely,' he'd said.

Miss Everest heard him and now Javin has to sit in Mr Dean's reading group as well. Javin said it might send Mr Dean there sooner if he had to put up with him every week.

Miss Everest said Mr Dean would love it.

'He enjoys a worthwhile challenge,' she said.

Now Mr Dean and Javin and Jimmy spend a lot of time going through old surfing magazines. Javin even asked me for one of my dad's art books that have airbrushed surfboards and motorbikes in them. My dad's not like Mr Dean. 'Not likely,' he said. So Javin never got them.

'I'm not doing it,' Javin said before Miss Everest even got a chance. 'I read with him every week but I'm not wearing a cow suit!'

'It'll be fine,' Miss Everest said and got busy reorganising everyone.

She's very good at it and makes everything sound so wonderful that all the groups were changed around about fifteen times before we had it right.

I stayed with the angels.

And Javin stayed with the shepherds. I don't know if he wanted to be a shepherd as much as I wanted to be angel or if he was just staying right away from the manger cow.

The wise men were happy and so was George, the innkeeper, except that he said he really didn't want a wife. Especially one that was a girl.

Miss Everest said it was best he did have one, in the kind of voice that meant the innkeeper might not be in the play at all if he didn't have one. A girl one.

The sheep group was empty. Not even Miss Everest could make walking around on all fours tied up in a fluffy bath mat sound wonderful.

And there was only Jimmy in the manger cow group.

'We need one more over here,' she said when she'd reorganised for the sixteenth time.

We all huddled closer.

I liked Jimmy. I was pretty sure that everyone else did as well. But we all knew how hard it was for Jimmy to remember things. He often forgot which way his team was chucking the ball, or which end was his team's goal when we were playing soccer. Shani even tied her hair ribbon around the goal posts one day because she really, really wanted to win the game.

'Red, Jimmy!' she said. 'Just kick to the red goal!'

She forgot to remind him to kick the other way after half-time and we lost by two whole goals.

Now he sat with the cow's head on one side and the cow's bottom end on the other.

'Never mind,' Miss Everest said. 'I'm sure we can sort it out later.'

We all snuggled down into our groups to start working out the right way to act.

Mr Henderson came down to help us practise. He stood very close to Miss Everest and every now and then had to lean over close to tell her something. It was supposed to be about our singing, but I think he was sharing other secrets because she smiled at him and nodded her head before she made her face all serious again and posed her hands ready to conduct us.

Some of Mr Henderson's class are going to be sheep. They're not very good at it yet.

'They all keep going the wrong way!' Javin said

the first time he tried to walk along behind them.

Miss Everest laughed. 'Just like real sheep,' she said.

Javin didn't laugh. I think he told the sheep where lamb chops come from, because they started to get better by the end of our first practice.

I was getting it right too.

I stood in the middle of the back row on one of our benches. I could stand as still as a statue and Miss Everest said I was the best at opening my mouth up wide when I was singing.

Serena and Angela stood on one side and Katie stood on the other. Shani and Carol stood on the floor at the end of the benches. They didn't want to be in the play and Miss Everest was not sure if they were going to come. Shani said she had to play in the soccer comp and Carol had to help out in her mum's restaurant.

We practised every week in our classroom for weeks and weeks.

We got very good at packing up and stacking our desks against the walls so we had our own little stage area in the middle of the room.

Mr Henderson would bring his guitar and his sheep and the not-sheep would bring their crayons and paper and we all got better and better and better.

Finally Miss Everest talked to us about our

costumes. 'You can wear whatever you like that will fit your role,' she said. She gave us some pictures of angels and shepherds and innkeepers and innkeepers' wives, and written instructions with suggestions about the sort of things that would look right.

I didn't really need the instructions. I was going to be the most beautiful angel that ever stood on the stage in a Christmas play.

Ever.

Chapter Six

Mum put the list of instructions on the fridge. I saw Dad glance at it while we were wiping up.

'We have to have them ready for next week,' I said. 'It's the dress rehearsal.'

'Right,' he said. 'Do we have to buy tickets for this show?'

'Next week,' I told him. 'I can take the money in on Monday. But we have to have our clothes ready for Wednesday. Miss Everest said we have to have everything ready.'

I stressed everything but he didn't seem to take the slightest bit of notice.

We'd been practising for weeks and I still hadn't

seen any sign of a costume, even though I kept mentioning it about a thousand times a day.

'Have you checked your roster?' Dad said to Mum. 'It'd be awful if they'd put you down to work late on Wednesday.'

'I'm right,' Mum said. She ducked Roly's head in front of us so we could give him a kiss goodnight. 'But you've got all that art work to be done for Dave. And the car's not done …'

She whooshed out of the kitchen with Roly. Dad followed her.

'But what about my wings?' I yelled after him. 'You said you were going to make some for me.'

They didn't even answer.

I could hear them talking to Roly and then tiptoeing back up the hallway.

'Mum?' I yelled again, a little more quietly. 'We have to have the dress by next week.'

I walked into the lounge room. They were not even there. There was no one to listen to a word I said.

'Will this do?' Mum was holding something on a hanger. It was covered with a green garbage bag. And Dad appeared with something else.

'And these?'

I could see what they were straightaway. He was holding them by two fingers to show me how light they were.

Wings.

Long cardboard wings covered in little fluffy feathers that must have taken ages to collect. And then longer feathers that trailed, one over the other, to finally end in glossy gold tips. Dad had even painted gold on the inside of the wings so they'd shine when I lifted my arms.

'Where did you get them?' I was almost whispering, as if it might frighten the feathers and they'd all disappear if I spoke too loudly. I wanted to touch them but they were so carefully glued I was afraid to disturb them.

'Over at old Mr Lucas's farm,' Dad said.

I reached over and gently touched a soft grey feather that swooned down to the deepest tip.

'There's a couple of bare-chested geese wandering around over there, but Mr Lucas said it was for a good cause. He's even coming to the concert to make sure you don't take off!'

I touched another feather. It guided my finger from its tip to its tail.

'I collected as many white ones as I could,' Dad was saying. I was looking at the small, pale blue star woven with silver thread that formed the centre of the wings. It looked familiar.

I leaned closer and I knew exactly where it had come from.

I heard the rustle of green plastic beside me and looked across. There, hanging in deep folds, was my angel dress.

It was beautiful. Even more beautiful than it had been when it was a sari.

'You cut up your sari dress,' I said.

'Do you like it?'

They were both standing there looking at me like kindy kids on show-and-tell day.

Mum was so proud she held the skirt wide and then let it fall to show me how she'd matched up all the little silver threads.

'See,' she said and held it closer to me, 'I've put all the little star designs across the top and I found some silver thread in the supermarket and twisted it to make straps. And here'—she pointed to the little tie in the centre of the front—'that ties across so it will fall in long folds right down across your feet. And look at the arms ...'

The cuffs were cut into long points that draped down over my wrists and caught, with another silver thread, around my middle finger. 'Just like a true medieval angel,' she said.

I wasn't sure what a medieval angel was. It didn't really matter. I just knew that my angel dress and wings were perfect.

'And we can pull your hair down flat onto your

head, like this.' Mum had hold of a handful of my hair. 'Hold up the painting, Dave.'

Dad opened the book that had been on the table. He held it in front of me. There, hovering above Baby Jesus and Mary, was an angel in a dress with sleeves like mine. Her face looked a bit odd and I didn't much like her nose. Mary's eyes didn't look quite right either. They seemed to be looking in the wrong direction and poor Baby Jesus looked too old to be a baby.

'Do you think I could have some curls?' I said.

'Do you really want curls?' Mum stood back. She was still holding my hair. My head went with her. 'Curls are pretty ... cutsey, don't you think?'

I decided not to say that I liked cutsey.

I looked at the painting. The angel could do with a curl or two as well. And so could Mary.

'Don't you like it?'

The blue angel dress shone across at me and the wings were so soft they quivered at their centre when Mum lifted them.

'Here. Let's try it all on and then we can see about your hair.'

The sari drifted over my head and folded over my feet like foam on top of a wave. It was so soft it almost melted as I picked it up to walk.

Dad tied my wings around my chest and

shoulders and I felt feathers warming my back.

'Do you think they need more gold paint on their tips?' Dad said when I finally stood in front of them.

I craned around to see. 'I'll go and look in the mirror,' I said.

I wanted to stand by myself all alone in front of the long mirror in Mum and Dad's room. I wanted to

turn one way then another to see how the wings looked from the side and from the front and from the back. I wanted to point my toes. I wanted to spread my arms and see how the sleeves clung in blue folds against my skin. I wanted to tilt my head and twirl around and around and around.

'You go and look while we make a cup of coffee,' Mum said.

As I walked up the hall I was so happy I thought I might actually take off. I tried one little skipping step but my wings became nervous and wobbled so much I had to stop.

Angels on clouds weren't supposed to thump along skipping.

I opened the door into Mum's room and the mirror caught me in its reflection.

An angel.

I stood perfectly still. I could almost hear the cameras rolling as I stepped one long pointed toe step closer.

I lifted my chin then had to put it down again so I could watch.

I lifted my arms and my wings shone, their gold tips like tiny exclamation points behind me.

I glanced behind me to make sure nobody was watching, then I bowed, long and deep, with my arms stretched out to the sides.

I was taking my bow.
The angel who was the star of the show.

Chapter Seven

My dress and wings hung on the outside of my cupboard door all weekend and Monday and Tuesday. They were the first things I saw in the morning when I woke up and the last things I saw at night when I curled up to go to sleep.

Roly screamed the first time he saw my wings and ran around the house saying 'bird, bird, bird' for about an hour, but then he was okay. He didn't come back into my room though and that suited me fine.

On Wednesday morning Mum slipped the green garbage bag over my dress and another over my wings to protect them so I could get them to school without them jamming in the car door or something.

She drove me all the way in so I wouldn't have to go on the bus, but I let the wings droop out the bottom of their bag so the kindy kids who hung around the gate could admire them.

Their gold tips glittered in the sun.

'Bye,' I called as Mum drove away. I waved and pretended not to notice the little kids looking at the feathers that bloomed out of the bag.

I could hear them whispering and one little kid was jabbing her friend and pointing.

I smiled as I swooshed past them through the school gate.

'Why are taking a chook to school?' said one little kid who wouldn't know an angel if it landed on her head.

'It's not a chook.' Another one bent over and tried to lift the bag. I moved it out of reach.

'Chooks don't have gold paint on them.'

'She could've put that there!'

'It's not a chook anyway. It's a goose.' She jabbed the wing tips with a grubby little finger. 'Ew! You've got a dead goose in your bag!'

A couple of other little kids were hanging around waiting to see the dead goose. They were even sniffing the air trying to find its pong. I swung the bag up over my shoulder and managed to bump a couple of them.

'We had a dead goose once,' a little boy told me. He paddled along beside me with a dinosaur puppet in his hand. It looked like it had been dead for a while as well. 'Our dog dug it up.'

'Nice,' I said and hurried a bit.

He kept up. 'How come you brought yours to school? Did your dog dig it up?'

'Did your dog dig what up?' Serena Sweetmay had arrived. She'd swanned over with Angela and Katie and they craned over the others to see what I was carrying.

'Oh, they're your wings,' she crooned. 'Let me see.'

Before I could stop her she lifted the green plastic and held the cardboard backing so the wings fanned themselves out in the sunlight. The white feathers gleamed and their gold tips glittered so beautifully that another six kindy kids came over for a closer inspection.

'Oh, look,' one said. 'She's got wings.'

'Put 'em on,' said the dinosaur boy. 'Let's see if they fly.'

'Yes,' crooned Serena. 'Why don't you put them on?'

I didn't want to put them on out in the playground with everyone looking. I started to slide their bag back on.

'They're so sweet,' sang Angela. 'Aren't they?'

Serena and Angela nodded slowly and looked at each other.

'Touch them, Katie,' said Serena, smiling.

Katie didn't.

But Angela did. She stretched out her middle finger and let the very tip of it touch the longest goose feather. 'They're real!' she shrieked.

'They're goose feathers,' I said. As if she didn't know. 'Haven't you ever seen a goose feather before?'

'Only on a goose,' said Serena.

Angela covered her mouth. She smiled, but her eyes were looking at Serena and then at Katie. I hoped goose germs rushed into her mouth and down her throat to make her vomit.

They didn't.

Serena pointed to our classroom. 'Come on,' she said. 'You have to put them away. I'm sure Miss Everest will love them.'

They led the way.

I stumbled along behind them. Two plastic bags full of goose feathers and cardboard and a dress on a padded coathanger and a school bag full of lunch and a couple of weeks of old notes were pretty heavy and I was puffing so much by the time we arrived I could hardly speak.

It was just as well. Otherwise I might have reminded Serena and Angela and Katie how rude it is to walk along in front of someone and have very private conversations as you went.

Especially if the someone that you were talking about was walking along behind you.

Chapter Eight

Miss Everest was already inside. She was busy with a couple of mums who'd brought in their little kids to be the sheep. They were testing out bath mats to see which ones were the fluffiest. The little kids just stood there while white towelling rugs and soft fluffy blankets were wrapped one way then another. They looked more like bleached chickens than sheep.

Jimmy was standing beside her.

'It'd be great, Jimmy,' she was saying. 'You can be the leading ram and these little lambs will have to follow you.'

One mum held up a bigger bathmat with a foot print on it. 'You won't even see it,' she was saying.

'Honestly.'

Jimmy wasn't listening. 'I really want to be the cow's head,' he said.

I knew how he felt.

I just wanted to be an angel and there was no way

Chapter Eight

I wanted to change. Not even to help him out.

'I'll be a cow's bum with you in another play, Jimmy,' I said.

'There won't be another play,' he said and sat down in the middle of the rug with the cow's head on his lap. It looked a bit lonely without its other half but not as lonely as Jimmy.

'We could make one up,' I said as I unloaded my lovely dress. 'Couldn't we, Miss Everest.'

'We could,' she said and patted Jimmy on the head as she went back to make sure her little sheep were sorted. The mums kissed them goodbye and left and Miss Everest slipped off her shoes so she could sit on her chair and admire our clothes.

'Let me see,' she said. She looked at all the clothes hanging from the window frames.

'My word.'

I looked around too.

The shepherds had old sheets and towels draped about and the innkeeper and his wife had wonderful striped outfits with cut-off pillowcases to drape over one of their shoulders. And then there was the angel's corner.

First I saw the wings.

A forest of swan's down floated on every breath of every whisper in our classroom. Tiny sparkles winked out and about from each tiny feather.

Invisible, beautiful dragon's wing colours that were quick to catch your eye and then gone in a blink. Wicked little flashes of red, then green then aqua and then the white of a summer sky at midday. Every colour of every ocean floor, of every star, of every living thing shone out of those wings.

And then I saw the dresses.

Long wisps of fabric that didn't look too happy to be dangled onto a classroom carpet. Long folds that turned from snowiest white to clotted cream. Necklines of satin that gleamed as softly as spaniel ears. Coat hangers decorated with lavender bags.

And above them, just loosely hung around the bent wire of the hanger, were halos made of invisible wire so they hovered in holograms of purples.

Beside them my goose wings sprang proudly out of their green garbage bag and my pale blue dress swung merrily, flapping its silver stars in the breeze.

'It doesn't match the others,' I said to Miss Everest. 'But it'll be all right. See, it's got a matching silver star on the wings. My dad put it there especially.'

'I like it,' Carol said. 'I wish I didn't have to help in the restaurant. I'd get Mum to make me a blue dress, too.'

Miss Everest held my dress up to the light. 'It'll be perfect,' she said.

Chapter Eight

And she tried really hard not to look at the other dresses floating on the breeze while they waited to be noticed.

She didn't quite manage it though.

'I'll be fine,' I said again.

'Yes,' she agreed. 'You'll be wonderful.'

But I couldn't help thinking that my dress looked as lonely as the cow's head that lay in Jimmy's lap.

Chapter Nine

We all stood in our costumes.

It had been a long walk from our classroom down to the hall and we had to stop a couple of times because bits of costumes kept falling off. George's tea-towel kept slipping one way when his face was going another and twice he trod on Madi's mum's best sheet which was attached around Madi's neck and she almost choked.

Miss Everest said that people don't choke as loudly as that and she should try to keep her sheet off the ground. She stopped us all while she tied George's tea-towel in place with another piece of cord. George complained that his brain was being squashed because she tied it so tight, but Miss Everest said there was absolutely no chance of that.

We all laughed, but by the time we found the hall keys and got the hall unlocked and filed in we were feeling quite tired.

'Now,' said Miss Everest, 'let me look at you.'

We stood perfectly still in one long line.

'Pretty good,' she said.

I could see our reflection in the hall doors. I thought we looked pretty good too.

The shepherds looked all shepherdy in old towels and sheets, and the wise men looked very colourful in their mum's old evening dresses. Simone had on her grandma's brocade jacket that she had bought in China. It's an actual Chinese jacket, so I told her that my angel's dress had been a sari.

'Have a look,' I said and held it out so she could see how the stars changed from being little clusters to long twists of flowers as they stretched higher. 'She bought it in India.'

'And it smells because it lived in the bottom of her cupboard,' said Serena. 'I saw it when my dad had to visit with Dan.'

I didn't much like Serena calling my dad 'Dan'.

I was going to say it was a pity that dumb old Dave didn't know enough about drawing to do his own stupid art work on his own stupid surfboard, but Simone was so busy dragging my skirt out to show Kelly that I couldn't.

Miss Everest was tying her sarong around Javin who said he wouldn't wear a dress even if he had a mum to get one from and had turned up in his dad's old surf-shirt. He said it was okay to wear a sarong because he'd been to Bali and all the best surfers wore them.

The kindy sheep looked fine and their bath mats and rugs and blankets covered them exactly as they should have. Miss Everest had stuffed their feet into woolly bedsocks and added some extra wadding to make them look more sheepish. They were busy skating around on the polished wood and I thought they looked more like washing in a wind-storm than actual sheep, but I didn't say so.

Jimmy was standing on the end of the line with the cow's head over him and the bum end and tail dragging along behind. He said the cow was really tired from standing around in the manger for so long, so it'd be all right.

Miss Everest said she thought it looked like it had been run over by the farm tractor but perhaps we could sort it out later.

Mr Henderson arrived with the non-sheep group and sat them against the back wall. They sat down so quietly with their backs straight and their hands in their laps waiting for the concert to begin that I

Chapter Nine

almost felt like doing a little dance so they wouldn't be too disappointed.

'Right, everyone,' Miss Everest said. 'Go to your beginning places.'

This time we had a proper bench to stand on. The four angels clambered up. I stood on one end and then there was Serena and Angela and Katie. My wings battered Serena and tangled in her swan's down so she pinched me, but it didn't hurt much. I stepped on her toe and I think that hurt her a bit more, because she bounced right off the bench.

She was going to punch me but Miss Everest said angels never punched anybody and to cut it out RIGHT NOW.

I beamed out into the empty hall. The non-sheep seemed far away, sitting down there against the back wall, but I could see their little faces gazing up at me. They weren't poking or jabbing or wriggling. They were just sitting ready and waiting like it was a theatre and the curtain was about to go up.

I could almost feel them holding their breath.

I tried to imagine the hall full of people, all of them gazing up at me, gasping at the quick little glitters of silver from my dress and groaning at the splendour of my wings.

'Right, everyone.' Miss Everest lifted her conducting hand. 'After three. One. Two. Three.'

Joseph and Mary started their walk across the front of the stage. Miss Everest hit the 'play' button and we all started to sing.

I sang loudly and strongly with my mouth wide open the way Miss Everest had taught us.

The music swelled out into the hall, booming so loudly and perfectly from the speakers it filled me to overflowing.

I lifted my head and knew exactly what it meant to sing my heart out. I had my head tipped right back and my eyes closed the way real singers do. I had to fight to keep my hands folded one on top of the other because they wanted to swing out wide and embrace the whole audience that I imagined watching me.

I didn't even notice Serena leave our bench.

By the time I opened my eyes she was gliding out the front and didn't stop until she stood in front of Miss Everest.

Her dress whispered along behind her like a little pet that knew to hover closely and not get tangled or it might get a really sharp kick. It whirled itself into a neat pool when she stopped.

Everyone stopped singing. They were watching Serena and she was pointing at me.

Miss Everest leaned closer and nodded.

'I think we have a problem, Mr Henderson,' she said. I think it's funny the way she calls him Mr

Henderson. I bet she doesn't call him that when they're by themselves.

'A problem!' he boomed. 'A problem from the best singers in the whole school?'

He hurried across the hall making a joke out of whatever problem it was that Serena had discovered. I didn't think I was the problem.

Miss Everest had moved me up and down the bench a couple of times and had finally put another chair on the end of the bench to make more room for my wings.

But now she was listening to Serena, who was pointing to her hair and then to mine. Serena has blonde curly hair, as do Angela and Katie, and mine is dark and straight.

But it was going to be curly tonight for the concert.

I started to raise my hand to say about the curls when I saw Serena lifting her dress and then pointing to mine.

Mr Henderson creased his brow and pursed his lips. He scrubbed his hand across his chin as if it were, indeed, something very serious that had to be considered.

Chapter Nine

'What do you think, Mr Henderson?' said Miss Everest in a voice loud enough for us all to hear. 'Should I put my blue angel right there in the middle. Serena is worried that Aimee doesn't quite fit.'

Mr Henderson looked at us. He walked all the way around us and he looked rather severely, I thought, at Serena. 'You can't have a middle if you only have four angels,' he said.

He walked to the back of the hall.

He bent sideways and he straightened up.

Everyone was watching him. They didn't take their eyes off him.

Except Serena.

She did, just long enough to smile a quick smile up at Angela and Katie.

Angela smiled back, but Katie looked at her toes and took a very long minute to straighten her dress.

'Do you know,' he boomed across the empty hall, 'I'd put the blue angel right in the front. Right there ...' He galloped up and stood right slap bang in the middle of the stage in front of everyone. 'In the very front where everyone in the audience can see her.' He turned around and addressed the non-sheep. 'What do you think?' They all cheered and said 'Yes'.

I cheered too. On the inside. But I think it beamed right out to the outside when I opened my mouth to sing.

I sang the loudest I've ever sung in my whole life. Even Miss Everest noticed.

And that was nothing to how I was going to be tonight. I was going to be the very best, the most important, the truest actor and angel on the stage.

And everyone, absolutely everyone was definitely going to see.

Because I would be standing right where nobody could possibly miss me.

Chapter Ten

By the time we finished our rehearsal and went back to our room and got changed and re-hung our clothes on their hangers ready for tonight lunchtime was nearly over.

I thought Serena and Angela and Katie would have been looking out for me to gloat all over themselves because now they had the back bench all to themselves.

But I didn't see them. Not until I went into the toilets just before the bell rang.

And even then they must have been right behind me because they were standing waiting when I opened the door.

They watched me while I washed my hands and then drifted closer as I started to leave.

'What?' I said.

'Where'd you get that dress anyway?' Angela said. She leaned back against the sink and looked at her fingers like she had something really interesting stuffed under her nails.

I thought she probably knew where I'd got it. Serena certainly did.

'My mum,' I said. 'She got it in India. Ages ago.'

'Smells like it,' Angela said. 'Smells like somebody died in it.'

'It's really rather nice,' Katie said. 'I like those stars and things on it.'

Serena leaned across her. 'You mean the things that float around because they've come unstitched?'

I don't think Katie meant that at all but she wasn't saying. She stepped back so that she was behind Serena.

'What are you wearing on your feet?' Serena sang sweetly. 'I've got some old ballet slippers you can borrow if you like.'

'I'm not wearing anything,' I said, but I was seeing my dress and the way it hung under the window in the classroom. The blue looked too bright and happy against the soft snowy whites, like the loneliest kid at a birthday party.

Chapter Ten

'Just thought I'd offer.' Serena smiled. 'Your dress isn't long enough to cover your feet, that's all.'

I wanted to look at my feet but I didn't. They were snugged away in their big, old school shoes now. I knew what they looked like, all bony toes and the knobbly little one that poked up when it should sit flat.

I remembered a picture in a book that Miss Everest had shown us. It was a drawing of the Little Match Girl before she dropped dead. Her dress hung down and didn't cover her feet either.

And her hair was dark and flat and straight.

I didn't want to but I thought about my wings and how they looked hard and angry and poked out at the world with mean, gold tips flashing in the light. Angels would never be allowed to fly in anything so harsh and heavy. They'd be dropping out of the sky like dead ducks.

Or geese.

'Miss Everest said my dress is lovely,' I said and thought how much I sounded like one of the little kindy kids just before they give somebody a big, fat shove to knock them over.

Serena turned the tap on and then turned it off again. 'She has to say that. She's a teacher and she's not allowed to say that your dress isn't good enough.' She wiped her hands through her hair and then leaned back against Angela. 'That's why we thought we should tell you.'

'Yeah,' said Angela. 'We're your friends and that's why we're telling you.'

'Telling me what,' I said.

'Come on.' Katie started to move away. 'We have to go.'

Serena didn't move. 'You can go if you're too afraid to tell her the truth.'

'It's not true.' Katie didn't leave though. I didn't want to stay there and listen and it would have helped a bit if Katie had left.

'Tell me what's true.'

'Your dress stinks,' said Serena. 'It smells like the bottom of a wardrobe and old shoes. It looks old and it's falling apart. It doesn't even fit you.'

I pushed her.

I gave her a really hard push right in the middle of her chest. She would have fallen over except for Angela who acted like a mattress when Serena went backwards.

She pushed me back and I had no one to bounce me up again except the wash basin. I got a bit jammed and before I could give her one more good push they were gone.

'You can borrow my ballet shoes if you like,' Serena called out.

I could hear them laughing all the way out to the

playground. I wasn't too sure about Katie but it's best to laugh if you're on Serena's side. And I don't think Katie wants to be dumped yet.

I dragged myself back out from between the basins and looked at the wet splotches on my uniform.

I sat in the toilet with the door shut until my face stopped being so red and my eyes stopped filling up with tears. I hate cry babies.

But every time I thought about my dress waiting for me, all proud of itself and hanging so blue and glittery against the others, my eyes filled up all over again. I saw my wings that looked so wonderful in my kitchen and so awful next to fake swan's down.

I told myself that geese aren't supposed to hang around with swans anyway. You never saw them swimming around together. If I was a goose I'd peck a swan right on the head.

Hard.

I saw my mum making my dress and how proud she was.

I saw my dad hanging out at Mr Lucas's farm plucking goose feathers off the slower geese.

I saw me looking like my dress, the one that didn't quite fit, in front of the whole audience.

We were both so wrong.

I stayed in the toilets a long time.

I didn't come out until Miss Everest came to find me. 'Didn't you hear the bell?' she said.

I took a deep breath. 'I'm not going to be an angel,' I told her in a rush before I had time to think

Chapter Ten

about Mum and Dad and old Mr Lucas sitting in the audience looking for his goose feathers.

Miss Everest said she was going to speak to Serena and Angela and Katie, and I thought she was pretty

clever because I hadn't said their names at all. It made me feel a little bit better but it didn't matter.

I said it wasn't their fault, I just didn't want to be an angel any more. I'm a bit like Katie and I wasn't quite sure what Serena might do if I got her into really big trouble.

'But there's no time,' Miss Everest said. 'The play is on tonight and I want you to be in it.'

'I'll be in it,' I said.

But I won't be an angel. I won't be anything that anyone will see. That way they won't look at me like they look at my dress. Like something that's too loud and too tatty and smelly and whole lot too showy for its own good.

'Oh, please,' said Miss Everest. 'What can you be if you're not going to be an angel.'

'I'll be'—I had to swallow hard so I didn't cry— 'I'll be the cow's bum.'

Chapter Eleven

'You're the saddest angel I've ever seen,' Mum said as we pulled up to the school gate.

'I'm all right,' I said.

'She's just nervous.' Dad gave me a bit of a shove the way he does when he thinks I need cheering up.

I didn't even shove him back.

All the other kids were rushing off to get changed in the classroom. I could see Javin's shirt flapping around above his head as he lined up the angels to snap it around their legs. I was hoping he'd snap it good and hard, but Miss Everest's hand snatched it away before it could get going.

'Are you sure about this?' she said when she saw

me come in. 'You look lovely in your angel dress and the wings are the best ones I've ever seen.'

She had to say that. I knew it now.

'No,' I said. 'I think I'd rather wear the cow's bum suit.'

Miss Everest didn't even rouse at me for swearing. She bent right down in front of me and was looking so deep into my eyes I thought she might cry.

'It's what I really want,' I said to make her feel better. I looked away though. I think Miss Everest would pick a fib when she's looking at me so closely.

She stood up slowly and drifted her fingers through the new curls that Mum had twisted into my hair.

'It doesn't matter,' I'd told Mum when she sat me on the stool and started spraying my hair full of foam. 'I'm not going to be an angel anyway.'

Mum stopped spraying for a moment.

'Of course you are,' she said. 'It's what you wanted. You'll be fine when you get there.'

She sprayed another cup full of foam on top of my head and started twisting.

'I won't,' I said quietly.

'What changed your mind,' she said?

'Nobody.'

Chapter Eleven

'Nobody?'

I knew she'd guess Serena sooner or later. She always gets it right. And she'd say I wasn't to let Serena rule my life.

She'd said it a thousand times before. And I believed her. And I always agreed. And I always went to school ready to dump right on Serena and Not Let Her Rule My Life.

But Serena's tricky.

It's not always easy to see if she's running my life or not.

And I'm never sure what Serena might do.

It's why everyone wants to be friends with her. It's easier. And safer.

It's why Katie wasn't game to walk away.

'My wings are too big,' I said before Mum could get going.

Mum went back to twisting in a few more curls.

'Your dad went to a lot of trouble to make those wings, Aimee,' she said. 'And they're exactly the right size. I showed you the picture and you said they were lovely.'

'They just feel big, that's all,' I said.

She popped a kiss on my cheek. A lump of foam caught on her nose and she went all cross-eyed to make me laugh while she brushed it away.

'Here,' she said. 'Let me help you into your dress

and wings so your hair won't get all mussed up.'

She gave me another quick kiss.

'You'll be fine.' She said. 'Honest.'

I made myself believe it so I could smile. But I knew I wasn't going to change my mind.

★ ★ ★ ★ ★

Chapter Eleven

'Aimee?'

Katie was standing looking at me. The other two were over in the corner trying to get their halos straight.

'I think your dress is lovely.'

She reached out her hand to touch one of the silver stars that rippled across the front.

'Liar!' I hissed at her.

I liked the way her hand snapped back. I stuck my nose in the air and walked right past her to the head end of the manger cow.

'Get up, Jimmy,' I said.

The cow's head wobbled to its feet. It really looked like a cow when you stood right in front of it. 'What are you doing?' it said.

'I'm getting in the back end, so hold still.'

I straightened up to unhook my wings. It was tricky and they wanted to slip right back and collapse onto the floor. I was surprised when they didn't. I was even more surprised when I saw Katie take them and hang them neatly on the window frame.

'You'll trip over your dress,' she said.

I ignored her.

Jimmy was so excited he kept turning around to watch me, and whenever he turned the back end went with him. I had to grab hold of him in the end because I was starting to get dizzy.

I unzipped my end and pulled the cow's legs up over my own and tucked my dress down snugly inside. She had pretty fat thighs for a cow, but I figured it didn't matter. Her tail swung right out wide, so I bunched a bit more of my dress under it.

I gave it a couple of test swings.

Katie giggled.

'Get lost,' I told her. 'Go and play with your little angel friends and leave me alone!'

I don't know whether she did or not. I was too busy trying to see how to fit my top end around Jimmy's bottom end and listen to all Miss Everest's instructions.

'Keep your arms here,' she was saying. Then, to the front end, she said, 'You're the leader, Jimmy. You have to watch through here'—I saw her fingers jaggle through the little eye hole in the neck—'so you don't go the wrong way.'

Jimmy was going the wrong way most of the time. I didn't want to think too much about that, especially when I was the one following him.

'We'll be right, Jimmy,' I said.

Miss Everest made us stand up and walk in two bits to the back door of the stage. I had to carry my tail over my arm so it didn't drag in the dirt. We had to go quietly so no one would see us before it was the proper time.

Chapter Eleven

I was the quietest of all.
I didn't want anyone to see me.
Not anyone.

Chapter Twelve

'Just remember, Jimmy,' Miss Everest said when we got to the hall, 'you have to walk behind the back row of angels and then in front of the manger and stand quietly with the sheep on the other side.'

The sheep were standing up looking red and hot, strapped in their bath mats with their woolly socks tied snugly on their hands and feet.

'So go slowly, Jimmy, won't you.'

We all walked silently across the stage and took our places behind the curtain. Jimmy and I weren't going on until the curtains opened and Miss Everest was staying with us until it was our turn.

I was listening to Miss Everest's last-minute

instructions while she zipped my back end to Jimmy's front. She left a little gap so I could see the floor underneath us as I walked along. I reached my arms up Jimmy's sides and had his bottom under my chin.

I heard a couple of kids laugh.

'Put your head down a bit, Aimee.' Miss Everest was giggling too. 'The cow looks a bit like a camel. It's got a hump in the middle of its back.'

I put my head down.

'That's better.'

I heard a few kids agreeing and thought that this was the dumbest, dumbest thing I'd ever done.

The silver stars on my dress were itching at my foot and I lifted my other foot to have a scratch at it.

I heard somebody behind me laugh and Miss Everest telling them to shush.

It was hard bending over and standing still, but bit by bit I could hear the others settling into their places.

I saw the floaty bottoms of the angel's dresses cream past and I let the cow's back leg kick out a bit.

'Get off!'

The angel belted the cow when she had to stop and haul her dress back on.

'Be quiet,' Miss Everest hissed.

Suddenly it was so quiet that even the slip of the

sheep's fat feet on the polished floor sounded noisy. It was like the whole audience was holding its breath.

'Here we go,' said Miss Everest. 'Good luck!'

I saw the shepherds' feet silently slip by. I saw angel's ankles because Miss Everest had told them to hold the dresses clear of the cow. I saw the glow of lights from the stage floor. I heard the sigh of the audience as Miss Everest hit the 'play' button and everyone started singing.

I didn't bother. What's the point of singing when the only thing to hear you is the bottom of the boy in front.

Jimmy was though. I glanced up enough to see the cow's head swaying to the melody and I could hear his voice loud and clear.

And then we were off.

Chapter Thirteen

I was okay to begin with. I knew what I had to do and I was doing it. Keep my head down and take small steps.

It was going really well.

Head down, step, step, head down, step, step ... away in a manger, no crib ... step, step, step ...

And then Jimmy stopped.

I didn't.

The cow's bum walked right into the cow's head as I nearly finished up under Jimmy's armpit.

'Stop it!' Jimmy turned around to hiss at me. So did the cow's head. 'Get off!'

I thought I heard a laugh.

Chapter Thirteen

'Get going!' I hissed back.

I gave Jimmy a shove. The cow jetted forward, head first, and the cow's bottom had to hurry to keep up. I skidded out wide on the corner to catch up again.

The cow's tail whacked the cow's head.

I heard more laughing.

'Cut it out!' Jimmy hissed as he set off again. Everyone was singing the second song now and Jimmy started up as well. He really loves Christmas carols, but he started in the wrong place and had to stop so he could hear the words properly. He had to turn around a bit then to see where we were.

I heard a sheep baa and the cow's head heard it too and set off rather quickly to get to it before the third song started up.

I had to skip and then jump over the end of Kim's dad's coat that Fiona was wearing as part of her innkeeper's wife's costume.

I heard very loud laughter.

It was coming from the audience and it seemed to be happening every time the cow started to move.

I stayed still.

I wasn't sure if the audience was allowed to laugh and I didn't want to be the one who copped it because it was my fault.

Jimmy didn't. He kept going.

At least he kept going until the cow's head got too tight and he was suddenly slammed back to the cow's bum. The stage floor is very slippery when you have soft socks covering your feet.

The audience was really roaring now.

'Stop it!' I heard an angel hiss at me and then felt an angel's foot jab into my side. 'Everyone's looking at you!'

I couldn't stop. Not right there. Not when the cow's head had set off again to try and reach the sheep who were baaing rather loudly now as they tried to steer us closer.

'Move!' I hissed at Jimmy. 'Go straight forward!'

Jimmy did.

It was a shame he'd forgotten about Miss Everest's old doll's pram. He'd pushed it four whole steps before a shepherd grabbed it and put it back.

Jimmy tripped a little and would have fallen except that I held him tighter with my arms and lifted him, just a little, so he was facing the right way.

The audience howled.

I think they liked it. I think they really liked it because this time somebody started clapping as well.

Then I saw Serena's ballet slipper. It jabbed sweetly out and poked at the cow's rump.

'Move.' She must have bent right over. 'The whole audience is laughing at you!'

Chapter Thirteen

I took three little swinging steps so my tail whooped from side to side slapping at the angels as we finished our stage walk.

The audience roared with laughter and I heard more clapping. Then, when we finally reached our sheep and our corner of the stage and stood as still as statues, there was only silence.

We didn't move until the curtain started to close. Jimmy felt it brush by him and stepped aside.

He was supposed to step INside. But Jimmy had stepped OUTside.

We both finished up on the wrong side of the closed curtain. Everyone in the audience could see us.

I saw it whoosh by our feet and I heard very loud clapping and a whole lot of laughing and lots and lots of cheering.

The cow's head turned around to look at me.

'What'll we do?'

I thought fast. 'Ready, Jimmy,' I said. 'It'll be fine. Just do as I say.'

Jimmy nodded and the audience went wild. The cow swayed its bottom and its tail swung high.

'Now,' I said. 'Walk, walk, kick. Walk, walk, kick.'

I could hear chairs scraping back as the audience stood up. I could hear them clapping the 1, 2, 3, so we walked to their beat.

It was a wonderful sound and we walked right

around the stage and back again, keeping time all the way.

But the best sound was the angel's voice when we got back behind the curtain.

'It's not fair,' she was wailing. I saw her foot stamp. 'It's not fair! Everybody was watching that stupid cow and nobody looked at the angels.'

Miss Everest was unzipping us. 'Does it really matter?' she was saying.

'What about that man who was coming to watch us?' I heard Serena's voice over the din.

'It's dumb!' Angela joined in. They were both leaning so close to Miss Everest that she had to fluff their angels' wings out of her face. 'How come a stupid, fat cow gets to be the star of the show!'

'Yeah!' Serena clambered forward again. 'That man wouldn't even be able to see us properly the way that cow was carrying on!'

Miss Everest didn't say anything at all. She was busy shearing the sheep and hurrying us back to our holding pens.

She grinned at us though.

I grinned back, but as I hurried along through the dark playground I could only think of Serena.

Maybe she really didn't know how teachers think. Not if she believed that that man was going to be there.

I could hear lots of lovely thoughts clattering

around in my head, most of them to do with Serena who didn't know everything anyway.

I hitched my cow's bum higher and draped its tail over my arm. I felt so happy I skipped a bit.

Somebody behind me laughed and Miss Everest caught up with me. 'You,' she said as I skipped to a halt, 'were the best cow I've ever, ever seen!'

And I believed every single word she said.

Chapter Fourteen

Miss Everest gave us all a cool drink and helped us change and pack up our costumes.

Javin was hooting around waggling his rear like he had a tail attached. He kept giving me a nudge every time he went past, but I didn't mind. I reckon he'll want to be the manger cow next time.

'I didn't see you!' Mum exploded into the classroom along with all the other parents. She had one hand pressed to her mouth like she'd done something awful because she'd missed me. Her other hand smoothed the curls that were cemented into a shape a bit like a bicycle helmet. 'And look at your hair.'

Dad pulled a couple of strands free. 'I was so busy looking at that cow that I missed you as well. Boy, it was funny! I reckon those kids deserve a medal. You've got to be good to make an audience laugh like that!' He was looking around at the kids who were still struggling to get their clothes into bags to see if he could see who had been inside the cow suit.

'They were good,' Mum said. 'I nearly died when they made the cow do that little dance at the end.' Her hands patted my head. 'And I'm sure you were wonderful, too, Aimee. I just wish I'd seen you.'

'You did,' I said.

'No.' She shook her head. 'No.'

'I was the cow!' I yelled it. I didn't mean to but it just burst right out. 'Me and Jimmy! It was us!'

'Yessss!' Dad did his soccer cheer. I thought he might have been going to rip his tee-shirt up over his face and dance around like he'd scored a goal, but he danced me around instead. 'I knew it. I knew I'd seen that back end somewhere!'

Mum shushed him but she was glowing. Her whole face was beaming like someone had lit her up on the inside. 'I'm so proud of you,' she said.

I could see her thinking about how much I'd wanted to be the angel and for a second the inside light was dimmed. 'You shouldn't let people boss you around.' She said 'people' but looked right across at Serena who was standing fluttering her eyelashes at a bloke in a suit. Serena smirked across at me.

I poked my tongue out.

'It's fine, Mum,' I said. 'I had the best fun.'

I was just getting warmed up to try and explain about the dress and the wings and how sorry I was that I didn't wear them when the man who'd been talking to Serena came over.

Miss Everest came with him and so did Mr Henderson.

She told us his name was Jeremy and that he wanted to talk to us about the cow.

'I'm the tail end and he's the head,' I said, pointing at Jimmy.

'I know,' said Jeremy. He gave Mum and Dad a card with writing all over it. 'I came here tonight to see if there was anyone to try out for some commercials we're doing.'

Serena waltzed by. 'Goodnight, Jeremy.'

'See you, Serena,' he said. 'Next week at the first audition. Now,' he said, 'let's talk about our cow.'

It turned out that he wanted us to take our cow act to be part of a pantomime for one of the big children's hospitals in Sydney. 'Everyone can come with you,' he said. 'Your mum and dad and little brother.' Roly was eating the school chalk and I don't

think Jeremy was too thrilled about taking a chalk eater with him, but he didn't let it stop him. 'We'll train you, but I don't think you'll need too much training.' He laughed. 'You were the funniest act I've seen in a long time!'

'Do we have to do an audition?'

'You mean like the others? Nope!' Jeremy smiled. 'You and Jimmy are a couple of naturals. You'll just have to do a bit of training for the show.'

He shook hands with Dad and Mum and gave us a whole heap of stuff to read over and then went to talk to Jimmy's parents.

Miss Everest was looking so chuffed I thought she might burst. She gave me a quick thumbs-up sign behind Jeremy's back.

Mr Henderson was looking pretty chuffed as well, but I think that was because Miss Everest had hugged him when we all came off stage.

We weren't supposed to see it. But I did.

'I really did want to be an angel,' I said as I collected up my wings and smoothed out my dress. 'Do you reckon I can wear them at home sometimes?'

'I reckon,' said Dad.

We drifted past other parents and kids and headed for the school gates.

'That's another year nearly done,' Mum said as she hoisted Roly onto her hip.

Another year of Serena nearly over.

I glanced behind me to see if she was still around. She was standing with Angela and she saw me and waved her fingers. 'See you in Sydney,' she called. 'I'll be down there for the auditions after Christmas.'

I couldn't believe it. Another year of Serena nearly over. A whole holiday with her coming up.

I wandered along behind Mum and Dad and then I looked back. I couldn't see Katie anywhere.

'Where's Katie?' I called.

Serena and Angela smiled across at me and shrugged.

I checked around the school gate but she wasn't anywhere to be seen.

It didn't matter really. Nothing mattered too much tonight.

I got to be the star of the show. Me. The manger cow's bum.

And tomorrow, if Katie feels like it, she could find me.

You never know, we just might finish up being friends … if Serena doesn't mind.

OTHER CHILDREN'S FICTION
by UQP

TO THE LIGHT
Pat Flynn

Shortlisted CBCA 2006

Being inside the wave is the ultimate for a surfer. A place where, once you've been, you'll never forget. A place where time and space are squeezed and bent like in another dimension. But once you're in you have to make it out.

You have to make it to the light.

ISBN 0 7022 3492 3

UQP

THE LEGEND OF BIG RED
James Roy

Bailey's Swamp is a lot of things. Beautiful. Secluded. Creepy.

It's also thought to be the home of Big Red, a giant and elusive fish, a true legend of the local area. And Barney and Liam are determined to find him. And when they find him, they're going to catch him.

But they're about to discover that there's much more to be found at Bailey's Swamp than some big old fish.

In this exhilarating adventure story, James Roy will take you on a journey more electrifying than camping in a thunderstorm, and more thrilling than a Nantucket sleigh-ride.

ISBN 0 7022 3528 8

UQP

HIGH HOPES ON SEA
Jenny Wagner

The Hope family live by the sea, in a house with its hands in its pockets and a tin roof over one eye.

Mr Hope invents wonderful new devices. Mrs Hope likes burnt toast. Marissa watches the waves and Dion listens to the whispers of the wind.

But when Mr Owen Mortlock and his brother Selwyn decide to build some apartments, everything is suddenly different. The wind goes away, the ocean vanishes from their windows, and worse is still to come...

But of course, there's always hope...

...and there's always a breeze somewhere.

ISBN 0 7022 3525 3

UQP